Jack's Job

by Robert Bridges
illustrated by Meryl Henderson

Core Decodable 29

Bothell, WA • Chicago, IL • Columbus, OH • New York, NY

MHEonline.com

Copyright © 2015 McGraw-Hill Education

All rights reserved. No part of this publication may be reproduced or distributed in any form or by any means, or stored in a database or retrieval system, without the prior written consent of McGraw-Hill Education, including, but not limited to, network storage or transmission, or broadcast for distance learning.

Send all inquiries to:
McGraw-Hill Education
8787 Orion Place
Columbus, OH 43240

ISBN: 978-0-02-140710-1
MHID: 0-02-140710-X

Printed in the United States of America.

2 3 4 5 6 7 8 9 DOC 20 19 18 17 16 15

Jack's job had a badge.

The bridge had a traffic jam.
Jack had to act fast.

Jan had a flat on the bridge.

Traffic did not pass Jan.
It had to stop.

Bridge traffic had to pass.

Jack got the bridge traffic to pass.